SPACE
EXPLORATION

Written by
Clare Oliver

Illustrated by
Rob Jakeway, Dud Moseley and Terry Riley

p

This is a Parragon Book
This edition published in 2003

Parragon
Queen Street House
4 Queen Street
Bath BA1 1HE, UK

Copyright © Parragon 2001

Original book created by

David West 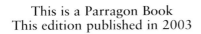 Children's Books

British Library Cataloguing-in-Publication Data

A catalogue record for this book is available from
the British Library.

ISBN 1-40540-280-6

Printed in Dubai,U.A.E

Designers
Aarti Parmar
Rob Shone
Fiona Thorne
Illustrators
John Butler
Jim Eldridge
James Field
Andrew & Angela Harland
Colin Howard
Rob Jakeway
Mike Lacey
Sarah Lees
Gilly Marklew
Dud Moseley
Terry Riley
Sarah Smith
Stephen Sweet
Mike Taylor
Ross Watton
(SGA)
Ian Thompson
Cartoonist
Peter Wilks
(SGA)
Editor
James Pickering
Consultant
Steve Parker

CONTENTS

❓ Who made the first rockets?

The Chinese made the first 'rockets' about 1,000 years ago, but they were more like fireworks than today's space rockets. They were flaming arrows that were fired from a basket using gunpowder.

Chinese 'rocket'

Amazing! You don't need to be a rocket scientist to build rockets. Lots of people make mini rockets as a hobby. There is even a yearly contest, when people show off their latest creations!

Is it true?
Thrust SSC is a rocket-powered car.

No. Thrust SSC, the fastest car, has two jet engines. A jet engine could not power a space mission, because it needs air and there's no air in space.

When did the first liquid-fuel rocket fly?

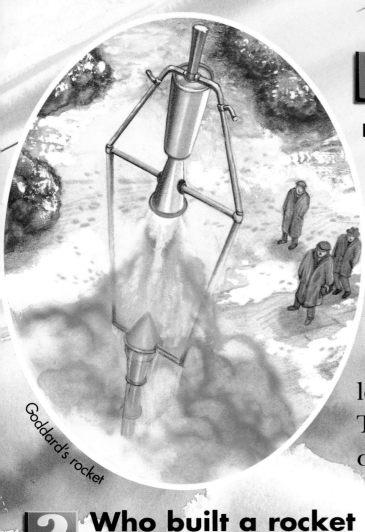

Goddard's rocket

In 1926, American Robert Goddard launched a 3.5 metre-long rocket. It flew about as high as a two-storey house, nowhere near outer space, and landed 56 metres away. The flight lasted just two-and-a-half seconds.

Who built a rocket for war?

Wernher von Braun invented the V2, a rocket missile used by the Germans in World War II. After the war, von Braun moved to the United States, to help with the new American space programme.

von Braun and V2 missile

? Why do we need rockets?

Rockets are important for space travel. They are the only machines powerful enough to launch things into space, such as satellites, probes and people. All the parts needed to build space stations have been carried up by rockets.

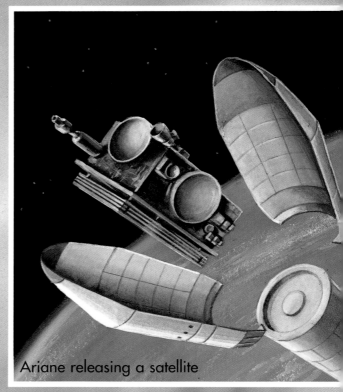
Ariane releasing a satellite

 Amazing! The European Ariane rocket could carry a fully-grown elephant. Ariane's biggest payload (cargo) so far was a satellite which weighed 4.6 tonnes.

? How fast can a rocket go?

To escape from Earth's gravity, a rocket has to reach 40,000 kph – almost 20 times faster than supersonic Concorde. Once it is out in space, the rocket drops down to around 29,000 kph to stay in orbit.

Is it true?
Saturn 5 rockets were as tall as a 30-storey building.

Yes. At 111 metres high, the Saturn 5 was the tallest rocket ever made. Most of the rocket fell away once it had done its job.

Saturn 5 rocket

Rocket stages falling away

? Why do rockets fall to pieces?

Rockets are made in stages, or pieces. Usually, there are three stages, made up of the fuel and rocket engines. Each stage drops off when its job is done. It takes a huge amount of power to push a heavy rocket into space.

Amazing! The first living creature in space was a Russian dog, called Laika. She made a seven-day journey in the space capsule Sputnik 2 in November 1957.

Voskhod spacecraft

Yuri Gagarin and Vostok 1

? **Who was the first man in space?**

A young Russian pilot called Yuri Gagarin was the first person in space. He orbited the Earth in a small capsule called Vostok 1 on 12 April, 1961. His journey lasted less than two hours.

? Who was the first woman in space?

The first woman in space was Russian, too. Valentina Tereshkova made a three-day space journey in Vostok 6 in 1963. The first American woman in space was Sally Ride, in 1983.

Valentina Tereshkova

Alexei Leonov making the first spacewalk

Is it true?
A chimp could survive a space flight.

Yes. Ham was the first to try out the Mercury capsule in 1961. Despite travelling at 8,045 kph, the chimpanzee survived the 16-minute flight.

9

? Who took the first spacewalk?

The cosmonaut (Russian astronaut) Alexei Leonov took a ten-minute spacewalk on 18 March 1965. To make sure he didn't float off, Leonov tied himself to his capsule.

Vostok capsule returning to Earth

? Which astronauts went to sea?

American astronauts returning to Earth landed in the sea and were picked up by helicopter. Their capsules had huge parachutes to slow down their fall, and rubber rings, so that they would float.

Amazing! Capsules got extremely hot. When a capsule re-entered Earth's atmosphere, its surface heated it up to 3,000°C – twice the temperature needed to melt iron. But they didn't melt, because they were protected by a special heat shield.

Apollo capsule splashing down

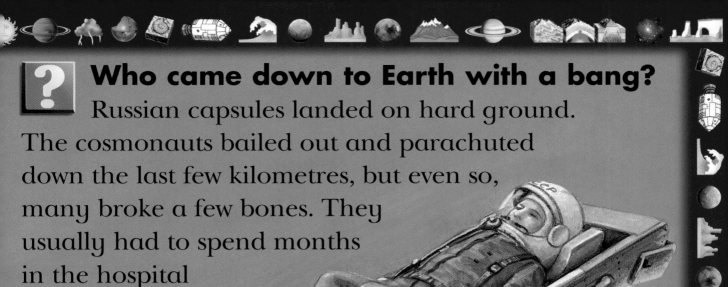

? Who came down to Earth with a bang?

Russian capsules landed on hard ground. The cosmonauts bailed out and parachuted down the last few kilometres, but even so, many broke a few bones. They usually had to spend months in the hospital recovering from the landing!

Cosmonaut ejecting

Is it true?
Voskhod 2 got lost.

Yes. Voskhod 2 was the capsule carrying Alexei Leonov, the first spacewalker. The auto-pilot machinery went wrong, and the capsule ended up 1,000 km off-course, in a snowy forest!

Mission Control

? Who knew where astronauts landed?

Machinery on board a capsule was radio-linked to Mission Control (the people on the ground in charge of a space mission). This meant people knew exactly where to find the astronauts – usually!

Neil Armstrong

Who first set foot on the Moon?

The very first person to step on to the Moon was the American Neil Armstrong, in 1969. He had flown there in Apollo 11 with Buzz Aldrin, who followed him on to the Moon's surface, and Michael Collins.

Amazing! There should have been seven manned missions to the Moon. Two days into Apollo 13's journey to the Moon, its oxygen tanks exploded. It took a nail-biting four days to bring its crew safely back to Earth.

Apollo 13

How many Moon missions were there?

There were six manned Apollo landings on the Moon, and about 80 unmanned ones too. Apollo 17 landed the last astronauts on the Moon in 1972.

Is it true?
There are footsteps on the Moon.

Yes. There is no atmosphere on the Moon, which means there is no wind either. Tyre tracks and footprints in the dusty surface will be there for hundreds of years.

Who first drove on the Moon?

In 1971, Apollo 15 carried a Lunar Rover. David Scott and James Irwin drove the battery-powered buggy over the Moon's cratered surface, collecting samples of Moon rock.

Lunar Rover

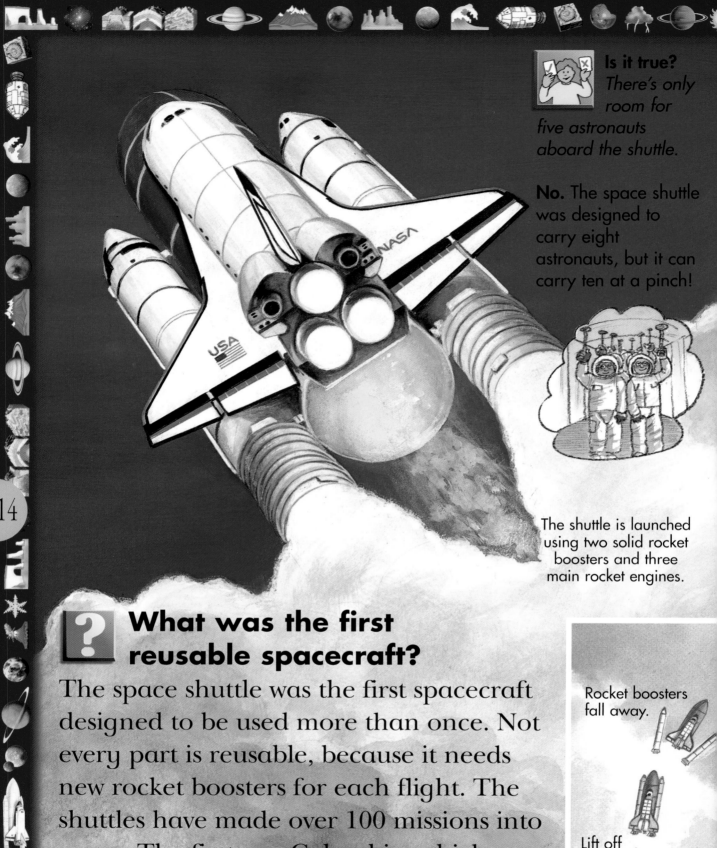

Is it true?
There's only room for five astronauts aboard the shuttle.

No. The space shuttle was designed to carry eight astronauts, but it can carry ten at a pinch!

The shuttle is launched using two solid rocket boosters and three main rocket engines.

？ What was the first reusable spacecraft?

The space shuttle was the first spacecraft designed to be used more than once. Not every part is reusable, because it needs new rocket boosters for each flight. The shuttles have made over 100 missions into space. The first was Columbia, which blasted off in 1981. It orbited the Earth at about 27,840 kph – about ten times faster than a speeding bullet.

Rocket boosters fall away.

Lift off

Challenger explosion

? How many space shuttles are there?

There are three space shuttles in use today – Discovery, Atlantis and Endeavour. The shuttle Challenger exploded shortly after lift off in 1986, and the shuttle Columbia disintegrated re-entering the Earth's atmosphere in 2003. Shuttles are used for launching and repairing satellites, and space reseach.

 Amazing! The Russian space shuttle, called Buran, only flew once, in 1988. Buran was carried into space by a rocket. Unlike the American shuttle, it was unmanned.

15

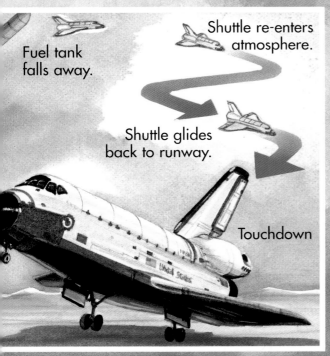
Fuel tank falls away.

Shuttle re-enters atmosphere.

Shuttle glides back to runway.

Touchdown

? How does the shuttle land?

At the end of its mission, the shuttle drops its speed to break orbit – on the opposite side of the world to the place it wants to land. Then it turns off its engines and glides like a bird, landing on a runway about an hour later.

? Why do astronauts wear space suits?

Space suits act like a suit of armour. They stop an astronaut's blood boiling in space, and reflect the Sun's dangerous rays. They have a built-in backpack, containing an oxygen supply, battery and cooling system.

Cutaway of helmet shows communications headset.

Amazing! Astronauts are water-cooled! A system of tubes sewn into the space suit carries cool liquid around to keep the astronaut's temperature normal.

16

Cutaway of space suit shows water-cooling tubes stitched into undergarment.

Is it true? *Cosmonauts took off in their underwear.*

Yes. In the early days of Russian space travel, space suits were worn only for spacewalks. Some cosmonauts just wore their underwear at take-off time!

Cosmonaut in space capsule

Do astronauts wear space suits all the time?

No. They wear them for spacewalks, and during take-off, landing or when they dock with another craft. The rest of the time, astronauts wear shorts and a tee shirt.

Backpack contains oxygen, batteries and water-cooling system.

Shuttle astronaut putting on space suit

How do you go to the toilet in a space suit?

Astronauts often need to wee during take-off! Women wear an extra-absorbent nappy inside their suit. Some men prefer to do this too, but others wear a special sleeve that carries wee to a storage pouch inside the suit.

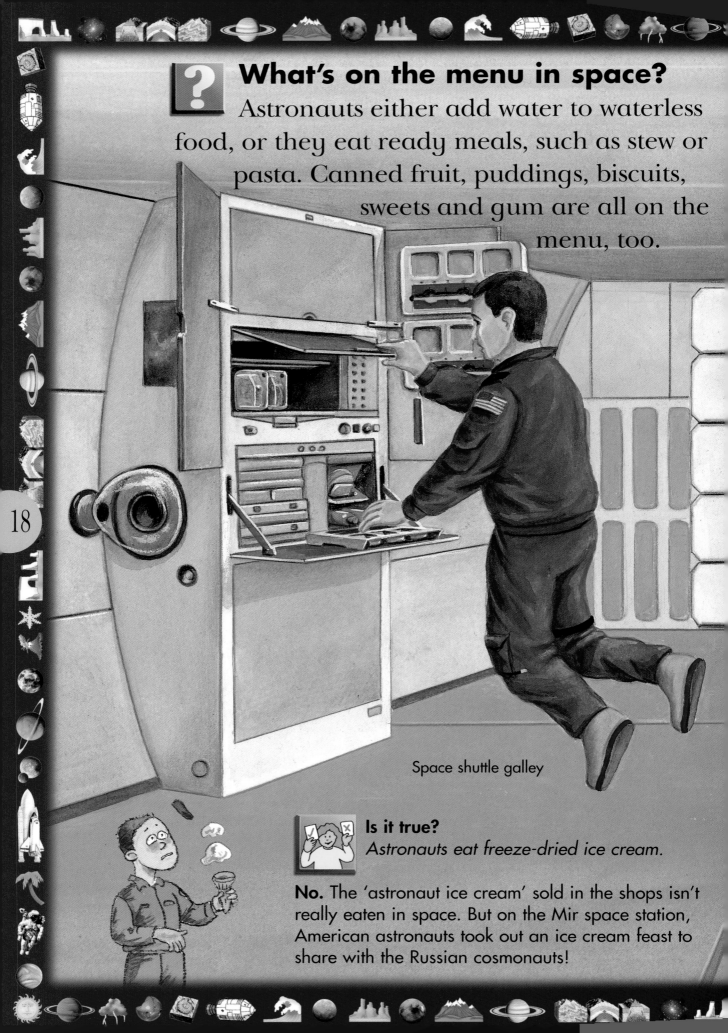

What's on the menu in space?

Astronauts either add water to waterless food, or they eat ready meals, such as stew or pasta. Canned fruit, puddings, biscuits, sweets and gum are all on the menu, too.

Space shuttle galley

Is it true?
Astronauts eat freeze-dried ice cream.

No. The 'astronaut ice cream' sold in the shops isn't really eaten in space. But on the Mir space station, American astronauts took out an ice cream feast to share with the Russian cosmonauts!

Eating in space

? Why doesn't the food float away?

Everything floats about in space, so meals are eaten from trays stuck to astronauts' clothes. Drinks come in a cup with a lid and are sucked up through a straw.

Amazing! Some astronauts get space sickness! Floating makes many astronauts throw up, and if they're not careful the sick flies everywhere! Luckily, the sickness wears off after a day or two.

? How do astronauts wash?

The Skylab space station had a shower fitted with a vacuum cleaner to suck off the water, but there's no room for a shower on the shuttle. Astronauts use wet wipes, and clean their hair with rinseless shampoo.

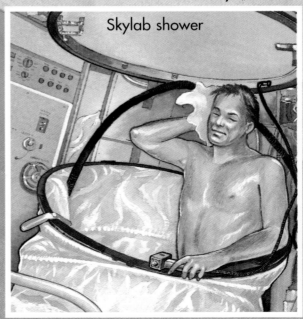

Skylab shower

Amazing! There were spiders in space. Arabella and Anita had a special mission on Skylab. Scientists wanted to see if space affected how spiders spin webs.

Soyuz spacecraft docked with Salyut 1 space station

? **Which was the first space station?**

The first manned space station was Salyut 1, launched in 1971, which had room for three crew. It was meant to go into permanent orbit around the Earth, but its orbit was a bit too low.

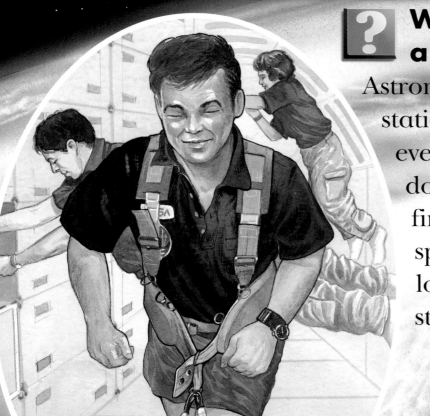
Exercise in space

? What happens in a space station?

Astronauts live in space stations for weeks or even months. They do experiments and find out more about space. They also do lots of exercise, to stay fit and healthy.

Is it true?
Your bones get weaker in space.

Yes. This isn't serious on short missions, but no one knows what would happen if you spent years in space.

? What's the biggest space station?

The International Space Station (ISS) will be the biggest ever space station when it's finished in 2003. The first module was launched in 1998 and the space station's parts are being built by 16 countries.

International Space Station

? Who needs a tool kit in space?

Astronauts need tools to build the ISS and repair satellites. In 1993, a space shuttle crew repaired the Hubble Space Telescope.

Working in space

MMU in action

? What's an MMU?

MMU stands for Manned Manoeuvring Unit. It's like an armchair that carries an astronaut around in space, when he or she is outside the spacecraft. It uses 24 little gas jets to move backwards or forwards, up or down.

Is it true?
The space shuttle has an arm.

Yes. It has a robot arm with a hand that can grip at the end. It can be controlled by astronauts inside or outside the shuttle. The robot arm is useful for picking up objects in space.

Amazing! Astronauts train underwater. Working underwater gives astronauts an idea of how it will feel to float in space. Water makes an astronaut's body move in the opposite direction when they try to pull or push something, just as it would in space.

Astronaut using headset radio

? How do astronauts talk to each other?

Space is an airless vacuum that won't carry sound. Even if they were yelling, astronauts outside their craft wouldn't be able to hear each other, so they stay in touch by radio.

❓ Has anyone ever been to Mars?

No, not yet, anyway! The distance from Earth to Mars varies from 56 million km to 400 million km. Even at its closest, Mars would be a six-month journey away.

Sun

Earth's orbit

Mars's orbit

Pathfinder landing

Is it true?
Vikings landed on Mars.

Yes. In 1976, two space probes called Vikings 1 and 2 landed there. During their mission, they collected samples and took over 3,000 photos.

❓ What used balloons to land on Mars?

The Mars Pathfinder probe entered the Martian atmosphere on 4 July, 1997. It used a parachute and rockets to slow down and then a bundle of balloons inflated around it so that it could bounce safely down on to the surface.

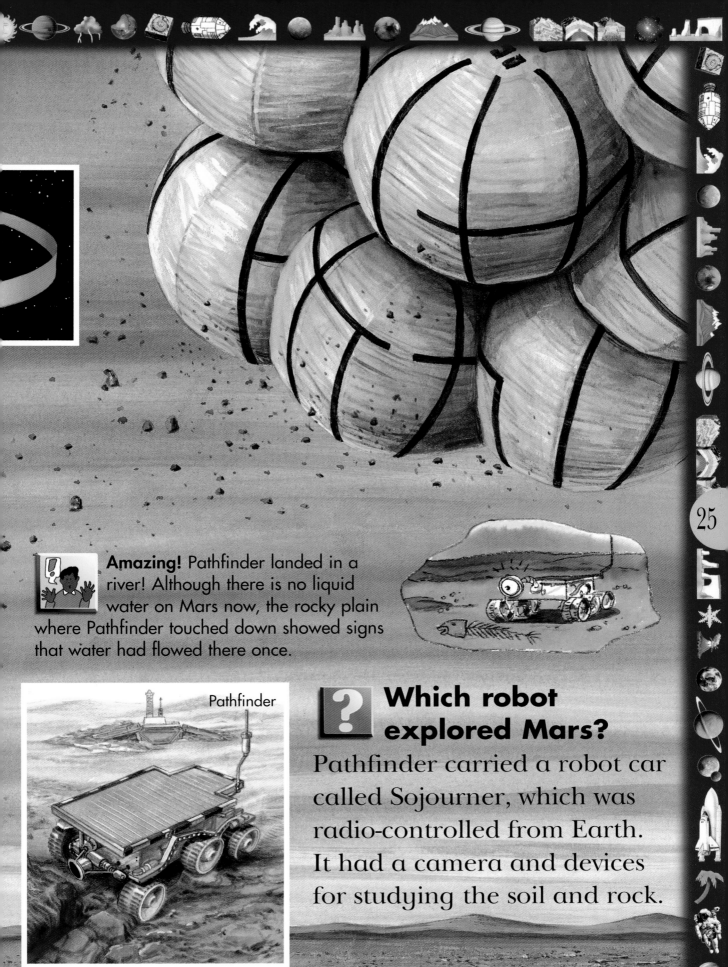

Amazing! Pathfinder landed in a river! Although there is no liquid water on Mars now, the rocky plain where Pathfinder touched down showed signs that water had flowed there once.

Pathfinder

Which robot explored Mars?

Pathfinder carried a robot car called Sojourner, which was radio-controlled from Earth. It had a camera and devices for studying the soil and rock.

What was the first satellite in space?

Sputnik 1 was the first satellite to orbit the Earth. It was launched by the Russians in October 1957 and took 90 minutes to circle the planet.

Is it true?
A person could have fitted in Sputnik 1.

No. The satellite was less than 60 cm across – smaller than most beach balls! Sputnik was just a radio transmitter really, but it was very important for space exploration.

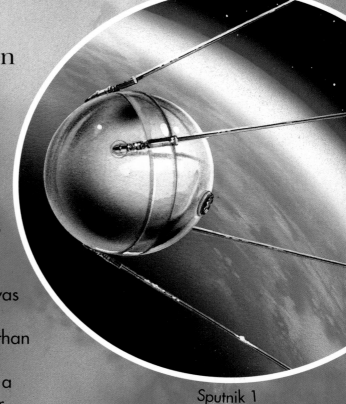

Sputnik 1

Can you see any satellites from Earth?

Yes. You can see satellites moving across the sky when the Sun is shining on them but it is dark on Earth. The best times to spot satellites are the two hours after sunset and the two hours before sunrise.

Amazing! Satellites are powered by the Sun. Rocket power takes satellites up into orbit, but once they're there, they use special solar panels to collect energy from the Sun. This is turned into electricity to power the satellites' batteries.

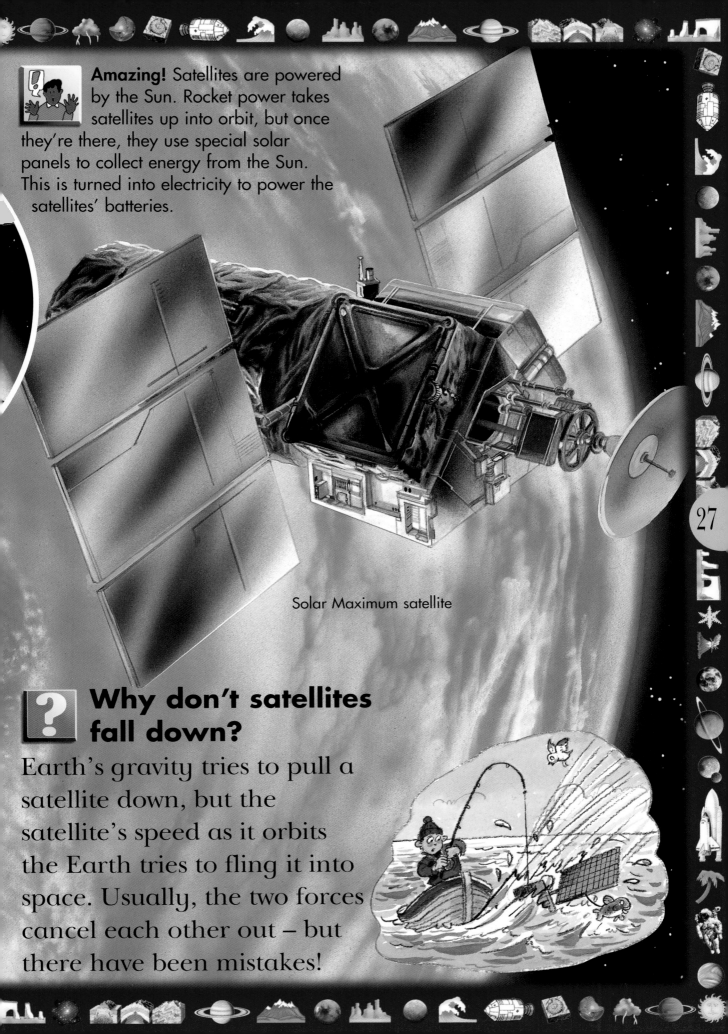

Solar Maximum satellite

Why don't satellites fall down?

Earth's gravity tries to pull a satellite down, but the satellite's speed as it orbits the Earth tries to fling it into space. Usually, the two forces cancel each other out – but there have been mistakes!

Which probe snapped a comet?

The Giotto space probe visited Halley's Comet in 1986 and took brilliant photos of the comet's rocky core. Even though Giotto kept a safe distance of about 600 km, its special protective shields got covered in icy dust.

Halley's Comet

Giotto

Amazing! A probe carries a message for aliens. The Pioneer 10 probe was fitted with a plaque, just in case it's ever found by aliens. It shows a man and woman, and a map to show where Earth is in the Universe.

Pioneer 10's plaque

Is it true?
A probe was made out of junk.

Yes. Magellan, sent to visit Venus in 1989, was made up of spare parts from other missions.

? Which spacecraft flew furthest?

Voyager 2, launched in 1977, has flown past Jupiter, Saturn, Uranus and Neptune. Now it is beyond our Solar System, heading into interstellar space.

Voyager 2 passing Jupiter

Cassini

? Which probe is as big as a bus?

The bus-sized Cassini space probe has another probe, called Huygens, on board. It should reach Saturn in 2004. Cassini will beam data back to Earth about Saturn's rings, moons and the planet itself.

Is it true?
We could never breathe on Mars.

No. We couldn't breathe in the atmosphere there as it is, but we could build airtight cities and grow plants there that would make oxygen for us.

Might there be pirates in space?

If we ever set up space mining stations, spacecraft would zoom about the Solar System with very valuable cargos. Space pirates might try to board cargo-carrying craft to rob them!

Will we ever live on the Moon?

Moon Base of the future

There might be a Moon Base, one day. The Moon is only three days away and its low gravity makes it easy to land spacecraft there. It would be a good place for telescopes, because there is no atmosphere to distort the pictures.

Amazing! People are planning a space hotel. Holidays in space are not far off. There are plans for a doughnut-shaped space hotel, using old shuttle fuel tanks as rooms!

Will we ever live on other planets?

It will take a lot more probe missions before we could consider building bases on other planets. But if travel to other stars ever became possible, the outer planets could act as useful 'petrol stations'.

Space tanker near Saturn

Glossary

Astronaut Someone who travels into space. The word means 'sailor of the stars'.

Atmosphere The gases or air surrounding a planet.

Capsule A small spacecraft with room for one or two crew.

Comet A body of ice and rock with a long glowing tail that orbits the Sun.

Core The middle of something.

Cosmonaut A Russian or Soviet astronaut. The word means 'sailor of the Universe'.

Data Information.

Gravity The force of attraction between two objects.

Missile A weapon that is thrown through the air.

Module A section of a space station.

Orbit The path around a planet or star.

Payload The cargo that a rocket carries into space.

Solar panels Panels of mirrors that capture energy from the Sun, and turn this energy into electricity.

Solar System Our Sun and everything that travels around it.

Stage A section of a rocket. Rockets usually have three stages.

Vacuum An empty space with no air.

32

Index